To Jim & Helen

from Alastair & Heather

with all our Love!

Prayers from the pandemic!

God of the Fallen Grain

ISBN 978-1-873739-37-2

Written by the Rev. Dr. Alexander Wimberly
Published by the Corrymeela Press
2021

The Corrymeela Community,
5 Drumaroan Road, Ballycastle
BT54 6QU

Original illustrations by Seán Harvey.
Typesetting and design by Studio Stereo.

Corrymeela is a Company Limited by Guarantee, registered in
Northern Ireland (NI006823), registered with The Charity Commission
for Northern Ireland (NIC101597) and registered as a charity
with HMRC (XN48052A). To learn more about the Corrymeela
Community, and to support its work, visit corrymeela.org.

Contents

Foreword

In these exquisite nuggets of longing—these prayers for our time
—we find a soul companion. We are guided in a daily pattern
of rising, and falling and rising again. Each poetic prayer leads
us first to reach out to God in all divine mystery; then to notice,
to question, to give thanks; and so to offer a response to the
world's brokenness, and our own, in humility and hope. This
is a beautifully simple yet profound pattern of prayer that has
sustained and upheld so many in these pandemic times.

Having first come upon these daily prayers online, I can now
savour each phrase, let each prompt surf through my soul finding
promise in the face of the profound ongoing pain of the world:
new hope in the midst of brokenness.

On Iona there is a granite sculpture named 'the Fallen Christ.'
Christ lies on the ground: a body broken yet strong, fallen yet
full of life. In recent months, with fewer visitors to the island
the statue has become more embedded in the surrounding soil:
grasses and mosses caressing the Christ as his cheek caresses the
earth. As with the fallen Christ, the fallen grain, so life longs to
burst through. As we falter, as we fall, so new growth emerges. It
is my heartfelt privilege to commend these prayers, these nuggets
of longing to you. May they caress your spirit and sustain your
soul through the seasons of life yet to come.

Ruth Harvey
Leader of the Iona Community

God of the Fallen Grain

Preface

As the coronavirus arrived in Ireland, I wrote a prayer. Then I wrote another. Then I got into the habit of writing a new prayer every day. Some were of lament. Some of petition. Some of confession. Most of them, to my surprise, ended up as prayers of thanksgiving.

I had no idea how long I would keep this up (maybe a month?) but I wanted Corrymeela to remain open in some way throughout the pandemic. Our residential centre closed temporarily. Our programmes moved online. Volunteers went home. Members had to remain socially distant. But these prayers kept our community accessible to those who sought it. The essential work of Corrymeela continued: welcoming people into courageous conversations where we increase our respect for each other and form a more hope-filled society for everyone.

If these prayers resonate, it is because they take part in that kind of conversation. That's why many begin with opposing descriptions of God: God you are *this* but you are also *this*. Can we talk about that? When these prayers have something worth saying, they speak to the wisdom of knowing that none of us is complete without the other. They argue that there is much more to learn from our differences than there is to fear. That we change the world by changing ourselves. That the planet needs us to be in genuine community with each other if we are to survive.

As the weeks of the pandemic became months, the beauty around Corrymeela changed with the seasons and provided ongoing inspiration. Ballycastle is a good place to quarantine. The sea, the glens, the tranquility of farmland, the busyness of town life: Corrymeela sits on the north coast of Ireland with an enviable array of views. The softness of spring gave way to the lushness of summer. The richness of autumn brought us to the harshness of winter. Over the course of a year, news arrived of spikes and waves. The trauma of this global ordeal seeped deeper into our tissues. People we love died. Others we love mourned. Many faced the chronic injustice of social systems not designed for them. Lockdown forced us to take an overdue look at the world we have created. At a loss for what to do, many of us gained new insights into nature's resilience and its built-in lessons of night and day, growth and decay, death and resurrection. Humbled by our interdependence, many of us gained new appreciation for the empathy and compassion that are as vital to us as water or air. That growth affected our prayers.

Spring came again, as it always does. Light returned. The seeds of last year's crop took root. But after more than a year of pandemic, we were not the same. We had lost much and discovered much. We had become a different community: wiser and wearier; shaken but surer of our need for each other. We found new ways to connect. We found ourselves linked to people around the world who chose to make these prayers part of a shared spiritual life. Ireland, Britain, the Netherlands, Germany, India, Indonesia, Australia, Korea, New Zealand, America, Canada: the spread of these prayers served as a daily reminder that although this pandemic separates us, it reveals our basic togetherness. Even in its indiscriminate destruction, even in its unwanted gift of death, this disease exposes a deeper truth about life's resilience, our primal need for human connection, and the enduring strength of hope.

God of the Fallen Grain is about hope. Hope that the seeds planted in this difficult season will bear good fruit in the future. Hope that we can face the painful realities of separation and death with a confidence in eternal and abundant life. Hope that we can transform our divisions and become a people who live well together.

Hope that tomorrow can bring, perhaps to our surprise, another prayer of thanksgiving.

Alex Wimberly
Lúnasa 2021

✝
✝

God of the grain that falls to earth,
God of the fruit that grain will bear:
you have created us to create life,
even as we lose it;
you have given us a gift of love
that grows the more we share it.
May we, as single grains of life,
not hold our love within,
but cast it wide
and lose ourselves
so new life can begin.
Amen.

Welcome

Respect
Courage
Hope

✝
✝

God of the guest house,
God of the room we prepare:
the ones we welcome
and the ways we welcome
will reveal a great deal
about how we receive
your good news.
May we, in this time
of social distancing
and human longing,
accept your invitation
to meet you again in the stranger,
and to meet ourselves in the
emotions we house,
and at the doors we either open
or close.
Amen.

✢
✢

God of the widow and God of the prophet:
you told us a story
of how a little oil and a little flour
and the kindness of community
saw a family through.
Jar after jar was filled and stored.
Remind us how a drop and a speck,
a tap on the door,
the willingness to believe in response to a need
made all the difference in that story,
and can make all the difference in ours
too.
Amen.

✝
✝

God whose breath hovered over creation,
God whose breath brought wet clay to life:
Be in each grounding breath we take,
the rise of our belly,
the fall of our chest.
Be in the kind word we extend,
the offer of help, the note of concern.
Be in the prayer that we whisper,
and the laugh that we share,
so that even in a time of chaos
we might breathe into life a new creation.
Amen.

God of the Fallen Grain

God of rivals, God of scapegoats:
we are quick to find someone to blame,
even when no one deserves it.
We look for ways to take care of our own,
while ignoring those most at risk.
We manage to indulge in just enough empathy
to make ourselves feel a lot better,
but we rarely choose to sacrifice
the idols we truly value.
Scapegoated saviour, as we muddle along
in this mess of being human,
allow us to see ourselves in the ones
we accuse or neglect,
and your grace in the place of judgement.
Amen.

16

✝
✝

God with us in difficult conversations,
God with us in difficult silences:
each moment and every mistake
gives us the chance to learn,
to understand and to change.
Before we react in fear or anger,
may we steady our breath
and calm our minds
to remind ourselves
that your love for us
is not in jeopardy.
And with that reassurance,
may we seek the truth
we need to hear,
and receive the grace
we mistook as threat.
Amen.

God of unbounded joy,
God of undying love:
the women went to the tomb
to tend to the crucified dead
and came back the first preachers
of resurrection.
As we come back from our tomb today,
and begin to live again,
may we deliver with unbridled joy
what the world is dying to hear:
that death is never the end;
that love remains what is most divine;
and that you continue to live
in the beating heart of our humanity.
Amen.

✝
✝

God of deeper conversation,
God of deepening relationships:
with so little known
about what lies ahead,
may we now take the time
to meet ourselves again,
and to encounter anew
the people we say we know.
These strangers who may be close to us
have more to share when we
open ourselves to renewed curiosity
and trust that undiscovered joys
lie within
the connections we already have.
Amen.

God of caught breath,
God of welcomed pause:
so much has happened so quickly,
that we can lose a sense of time.
As we continue to pace
and prepare ourselves
for more unknown to come,
we are grateful
for the faithfulness you promise:
the 'strength for today and
bright hope for tomorrow'
that we find morning by morning.
Give us that song.
Have us hum it by heart.
May we share the new mercies we see.
Amen.

✝
✝

God of friends, God of enemies:
perhaps the great act of faith these days
is not a belief in you,
but a belief that you are present
in the people we want to turn away.
Help us discover
that there is always more to love
when we see others as you do;
there are differences not just to tolerate,
but to celebrate.
As you have remained with us and for us
despite all we have done to withdraw,
may we remain with and for others,
judging not as you could judge,
but loving more than we deserve.
Amen.

God of the Fallen Grain

God of daily bread,
God of simple pleasures:
we ask for enough for today.
Help us give ourselves
the very thing we need:
a walk to clear the head,
a phone call that draws a familiar voice,
a brief exchange with a passer-by,
a gentle word of encouragement.
These little things and their significance
can be easily dismissed,
but it is often the non-grand gesture,
or an everyday routine,
or an in-the-moment whim
that reminds us that our God
was always there.
Amen.

✝
✝

God of earth's effortless turning,
God of this cycle of seasons:
one day on the calendar marks
both the beginning of autumn
and the beginning of spring;
the end of the north's summer
and the end of the south's winter.
While distant from each other,
we are connected by a rhythm,
a push and pull of light.
May it remind us that our journey
is not one we take alone,
and that the darkness we enter
cannot stop the coming dawn.
Amen.

God of the Fallen Grain

God of each breath,
God of this next breath:
may this moment we're in
be a moment now filled
with reassurance and grace;
with kindness and patience
for ourselves and for others.
May it be marked by hope
and compassion,
by learning and unlearning.
May it be a moment unencumbered
by mistakes we've made
or results we fear.
May it be a moment of peace
and renewal; a breath of new life.
Amen.

✝
✝

God with those on the margins,
God with those on the edge:
as we confine ourselves to what we know
and retreat into spaces we deem safe,
remind us that we are less likely
to find you there.
We will find ourselves alone
with the idols we carve and coddle,
and miss the chance to
touch your hem
as you head out to those in need.
But even as we fold ourselves
into our comfy pockets,
your grace doubles back to find us
and, with a cut, reveals
the edge we stand against
when we see ourselves as central.
Amen.

God of the Fallen Grain

God of our hearts and minds,
God of our nervous systems:
as our eyes and ears try to take in
another day of news,
our little bodies absorb the shock
of the biggest event of our lives.
Help us make sense
of what we honestly feel.
Fear. Loneliness. Exhaustion. Anger.
And in naming what lives in
our most inner selves,
may we grow more human
with each other:
warm-blooded and social,
communicative and relational,
present to nurse, eager to soothe
the people we more fully can be.
Amen.

✝
✝

God whose face is never seen,
God whose image shall not be made:
you knew – even before we
melted our gold to worship a beast—
that we would be quick to put
our face, our skin, our accent, our culture
up on a throne and call it your name.
Save us from this idol that we want.
Remind us that you are not
the best version of us, so that we might
rank ourselves in second place.
Show us again that to be divine is not
to reign supreme, but to relinquish power,
to empty one's self in love.
May we find you again alive in community
rather than lifeless in our reflection.
Amen.

God of the Fallen Grain

God in the welcome
that lets all feel at home,
God in the courage
that lets us let go:
if and when we know we are loved,
we can feel comfortable
in our own skin;
at peace in whatever turmoil arises;
and able to step out
into the unknown.
We will know that no matter
what may occur,
what is true will endure:
God will be.
Love will win.
And we will be with God.
Amen.

✝
✝

God of pilgrims who share this journey,
God of travellers upon this road:
this path changes us.
The conversations we have,
and the views we've gained;
the hurt we've endured,
and the muscles we've trained:
they bring us to a new place,
and to a newer sense of us.
As we unpack
the things we've carried
and recount the things we've lost,
may we marvel again
at the journey itself,
the gift of walking with others
along a path that takes us
into and beyond ourselves.
Amen.

God of the Fallen Grain

Welcome
Respect
Courage
Hope

✝
✝

God in our conflict,
God in our learning:
to be human is to find ourselves
in relation to those
with different goals, different needs,
different ways of being.
Remind us that our disagreements
are not the end of our connection.
May our differences
inspire our curiosity.
May our questions lead us
into better conversations,
letting us see the world through
others' eyes.
Amen.

God of the Fallen Grain

God of the prodigal's return,
God of the rivals' reunion:
when the son neared his father,
he bowed as a servant
and relinquished all familial rights.
It was the same gesture Jacob made
when he came near Esau in fear.
Their repentance and humility
were immediately engulfed
in a full-bodied embrace,
into a restoration of what was lost,
and a fuller celebration of what was found.
As we return to patterns
of work and life, and find ourselves
face to face again,
may we be restored with all
our humility and repentance intact.
Amen.

✝
✝

God of those who hunger and thirst,
God of the ones we imprison:
you meet us in the lives of others.
Too often we seek you by pulling away,
by retreating into ourselves
or by assembling some body
of like-minded souls. And yet,
the way to find you
is not in separating ourselves
one from another,
but in seeking your presence
alive in encounter;
in meeting the needs
of the people before us:
the ones in your family
we've sought to exclude.
Amen.

God of the Fallen Grain

God of humility,
God of courage:
each conversation we enter,
if honest and meaningful,
will expose a vulnerability.
We share our life experiences,
the good and bad, and open up to pain.
We reveal our ignorance of things,
both consciously and not.
And so we pray for your grace
to be with us
in these imperfect conversations.
For acknowledging our weaknesses
will reveal your loving strength;
and facing our fears together
will lead to something better.
Amen.

✝
✝

God of the one and God of the whole:
be with those who are working from home today
and those whose work keeps them from home.
Be with those who won't go beyond the front porch,
and those who stay on the front line.
Be with those who must choose between
doing a job they know they can do
and being the parent only they can be.
May we each in our private worry
hear your universal call
to come, to lay down heavy burdens,
and find a welcome rest.
And then with our burdens lightened,
may we help to hold the whole.
Amen.

God of the Fallen Grain

✝
✝

God of our great ideas,
God of our better angels:
when we are sure that we are right,
and that our solution is the best,
warn us of the danger that we pose.
Often, the insistence on one way
will make it harder for others to agree,
particularly when we think
ours is the only answer that makes sense.
Help us as we choose to let go
of what we might want to impose,
so that in the space that opens up
a co-created possibility might emerge.
And then help us see
that what is mine
is hardly ever as nice
as what is ours.
Amen.

✝
✝

God of every living creature,
God of every creeping thing:
a bird came into our garden,
and we didn't know its name.
The common snipe, the internet said.
'Common,' which suggests
our grandparents would have known,
and their grandparents too.
When did we forget it's normal
to see and hear nature on our doorstep,
and to appreciate the everyday?
Now that we've been stopped
by this common threat,
may we never let such knowledge,
or such birds, become so rare.
Amen.

✢
✢

God of rolling waters,
God of ever-flowing streams:
the skies do seem clearer,
and the air cleaner,
and the world less littered with our mess.
The earth looks more itself these days,
its resilience on fuller display.
But human nature is also more evident
and your warning rings loud in our ears:
what comes out of our mouths can defile;
what rots in our hearts can corrupt.
May justice and righteousness bathe us,
and wash out our self-serving sin.
Let us then resume our part in creation
and breathe out the joy we breathe in.
Amen.

✝
✝

God of the community well,
God of our individual needs:
we will draw from these days
a shared experience for years and years.
Yet each of us balances
this pandemic's challenge
with private struggles and
dissimilar circumstances.
May we take into account
the additional weight
that we and our neighbours will carry,
so that as we lend
each other support
we can draw out more lessons
from this well of community,
and bring home all that we can.
Amen.

✝
✝

God of those who agree with us,
God of those who don't:
keep us from dividing the world
into us and them,
for or against,
good and bad.
Remind us that humans
and human systems are always
more complex than the binary
choice of on/off, up/down.
As you have met us in the reality
of a living, breathing human life,
may we meet each other again
as three-dimensional people
and not as another yes or no.
Amen.

✝
✝

God of those in plenty,
God of those in want:
this disease separates us
one from another.
It also exposes an underlying division
that has been there all along:
the difference between the haves
and the have-nots.
May the chasm finally close between
those who will wait this pandemic out
with stockpiles of reserves
and the luxury of rest,
and those who have been waiting too long
for a voice at the table,
a seat at the banquet,
a prayer that
isn't filled with pleas.
Amen.

God of the Fallen Grain

✝
✝

God with us in a year of separation,
God with us in a future of reconciliation:
you tell us that your story
is incomplete without our story.
So may we resist the temptation
to separate our story from others',
or to listen only to tales that make us
hero or victim.
May we gladly hear a fuller story,
told as much in the lives
of those we call other:
those we have hurt without knowing,
those whose hurts we have failed
to acknowledge.
And then may we see ourselves
as part of the life
you alone can bring to completion.
Amen.

✝
✝

God of the histories we tell,
God of the histories we don't:
on either side of a border, you are there.
May we, in living out our faith,
never pretend that there is a way
to make ourselves purer,
or more righteous,
or holier
by separating ourselves from those
that you
will never stop loving.
Amen.

God of the shared bread
and the common purse:
you broke bread with those
who broke your trust and took
more than they needed for themselves.
You still do.
May our shared response
to a common threat
lead us each to reconsider
what we need and what we want,
and how we divide what we have.
Break who we are
so that we can be more for others.
Amen.

†
†

God of the crowds crying, 'crucify!'
God on the cross crying, 'forgive them':
by doing and not doing,
we have repeated that Friday scene
in countless ways,
in countless places,
to countless sons and daughters.
We know not what we do
even when we know too well.
We are now facing death in a new way.
And human frailty. And human need.
And human solidarity.
Perhaps as we begin to see as you see
the reality of who we are,
we can finally begin to love as you love,
answer compassionately the cries we hear,
and be able to forgive ourselves.
Amen.

God of the common ground,
God of the space between:
a renewed spirit of community
has been at work these many weeks.
We rejoice in this even as we know
that conflict remains part
of what it means to be human.
As we arrive at honest disagreement,
may we not seek
blindly to impose
our solutions upon others
(even if we know we're right).
Instead, may we listen and learn
from those we oppose
and look for more of
your answer
in the ground we give way.
Amen.

✝
✝

God of descending fire,
God of Pentecostal streets:
transform us into your people.
May we listen to those who speak
in the global language of protest --
shouts that are mistaken as foreign.
Their tongues/our tongues
tell of pain and fear
in words we all know by heart.
Send us out from our hiding
to speak about love,
to demonstrate the power of justice.
And may we see
the new community you make
in the admission
and forgiveness
of sin.
Amen.

God of the Fallen Grain

Welcome
Respect
Courage
Hope

✝
✝

God of big hills to climb,
God of little steps of courage:
help us light a candle in the darkness
and begin this journey
with renewed hope.
You know of the valleys
and the false summits ahead,
and the pasture that waits
with still waters.
Lead us on through the night
though we know there may be danger,
for we cannot remain where we are.
Amen.

God of the Fallen Grain

God of the seed and God of the branches:
you promised that a grain of faith
would be enough to move a mountain,
or better yet,
to make a nest for roosting.
May we now see the ripe fruition
of seeds planted long ago
by grand, motherly types
who sang us hymns we still can hum,
who showed us kindness
and quiet strength.
May we then grow in this new season
to plant a mountain-moving seed ourselves,
a shelter for tomorrow's wings.
Amen.

✝
✝

God of pastures and God of lambs:
these new-born creatures of spring
know nothing of the worry
or anxiety of our last month.
They know instead of
the earth beneath them
and the sky above,
and a mother who cares for them daily.
May we who know community
remind each other of
the steadiness of your providence,
the instinct in your protection,
the simplicity of your love.
And may we then with confidence
find our footing in this new-born world.
Amen.

God at the bedside, God at the graveside:
in care homes and hospices,
in hospital wards,
your spirit remains present
when family cannot be near.
With a comforting word or silent prayer,
in the final minutes of breath,
you have spoken a message of peace
through nurses and doctors,
chaplains and priests:
a Samaritan response at this roadside.
We give thanks that even if a disease
would rob us, through separation,
of a healing moment at death,
you appear at our side, time and again
with embodied, miraculous life.
Amen.

✝
✝

God of those we've lost this year,
God of what we've found:
our grief speaks to the beauty of life
and the toll that comes
at the end of each connection.
Death can offer a lesson
to the lasting goodness of life,
a pain that means that love is real.
May we never forget
that our grief gives proof of something
that was and continues to be true:
that our hope endures
in being held by your undying love.
Amen.

God of the Fallen Grain

✝
✝

God of our healthy fears,
God of our courage and faith:
there is a strengthening pull
wanting to carry us
back to what they call normal.
But there is also cautious resistance
and a reluctance to embrace all that was.
Help us in this in between.
As we venture out
and relax restrictions,
may we not forget the dangers,
nor lose sight of what we've gained
in a time of self-imposed limitation.
Strengthen our patience
to let this play out;
and may the lessons we carry
help us all to pull through.
Amen.

✝
✝

God of grieving,
God of silence:
there is a strange gift in having time,
one whole day this holy week,
to sit with questions of why and how long
and to hear no response at all.
To rush from Friday to Sunday,
from death to resurrection,
wouldn't do either justice.
Nor would it dignify the life of those
whose daily pain and grief
and constant pleas for justice
go unanswered in the world's daily rhythm.
Let your silence fill this silence,
until our empty noise dies out.
Amen.

✝
✝

God of the spaces between us,
God of the fractures within us:
in the gap between what is
and what should be
there is room
for empathy and learning.
There are truths there we don't yet see
but could come to understand
if we care enough to ask,
if we imagine the reality of others,
if we have the courage to change.
May we enter that space
knowing well you are there,
waiting for us to join you
in a recreation of what was empty
into a garden full of life.
Amen.

✝
✝

God of stilled waters,
God of calmed seas:
on a night of a difficult crossing
as your friends began to lose faith,
you awoke and hushed
the turbulent waves
with the power of unearthly peace.
May we respect the sheer force
of what we cannot control
and believe in the strength
that sleeps in this storm.
Amen.

God of the Fallen Grain

✝
✝

God of our finite selves,
God of our inward life:
unable to venture out,
our worlds could grow much smaller.
And yet
our path with you
can also lead
deep into our inmost parts,
to knitted secrets
we have yet unwound,
and to hidden thoughts
that you have loved.
Give us courage to explore
these darker, personal realms,
so that the broader peace
we hope to build
might rest on a peace within.
Amen.

✝
✝

God with us in our individual struggles,
God with us in our common ordeals:
there is a freedom that comes in knowing
that life is simply hard;
not because we've done something wrong,
or because we fail to see
something obvious to others,
but simply because life itself is hard.
May that never become the licence
to devalue another person's hardships
or the invitation to let our fears
fill the space that opens up.
May it become instead a moment
to marvel at your gift
of unconditional love;
the security that provides us with
a confidence not our own.
Amen.

God of the Fallen Grain

God of eternal life,
God of letting go:
throughout this long season
and over a century of days,
you have remained constant
as we've rediscovered ourselves.
There is more change ahead.
This pandemic is not finished.
Nor are we.
As we continue to be transformed,
may we cling to kindness and mercy;
to courage and trust;
to faith and hope;
to undying selflessness.
May divine love be made flesh
and given breath
in the life that changes with you.
Amen.

✝
✝

God of lifelong companions,
God of sudden discoveries:
we know that to be honest with others
risks pushing them away;
we know that their honesty with us
will show what we would hide.
Let our relationships be
the process of our becoming,
so that we are shaped
by laughter and tears,
by squabbles and smirks,
by courage and comfort,
by another who sees us
better than we can.
Amen.

God of our protective impulses,
God of the common good:
help us
as we make decisions in the dark
that will affect not just ourselves
but those we love
and those we should love.
Give us the courage to trust
not just our primal instincts,
but the good news
that what is best for the whole,
for the neighbour and the stranger,
is what protects the best in ourselves.
Amen.

✝
✝

God of a deep and deepening peace,
God of a calm that steadies our pace:
may we
take whatever moment we need
to gather ourselves
for the journey ahead.
May we feel the rock
of your presence beneath us;
the assurance of shelter
you provide in embrace;
and the promise of company
gathered close by your spirit;
so that as we approach
the unknown ahead
we remember a strength
that can never give way.
Amen.

Respect

Courage

Hope

✝
✝

God of the dust to which we return,
God of the ash that enriches the soil:
there are seeds from trees
that open
only after a fire has passed through.
They push the tips of their roots down
when the sunlight above has space.
May we remember
that after all we see passes away,
the gifts you promise remain.
Faith. Hope. Love.
And the greatest of these
is taking root now
in the soil of compassion and kindness.
Amen.

God of this shared earth
and this shared experience:
may this great leveller of a disease,
this reminder of our common fragility,
our mortality,
and our recognisable fears,
be also the great correction
in our collective story.
May this be the moment
when we start again
with clearer eyes and kinder hearts,
and with renewed resolve
to do justice, love mercy
and walk humbly
together.
Amen.

✝
✝

God of the home and God of the pilgrim:
we begin to dig in for an uncertain season,
and embark on a journey together.
This is a path we haven't been on.
Yet we know in each step
you are there alongside us:
a guide, a protector, a friend.
May each day on the road bring us closer together
closer to a land of grateful reunion
closer to the place you call home.
Amen.

God of the Fallen Grain

✝
✝

God who holds us in our brokenness,
God whose healing makes us whole:
the biggest event of our lives
is still unfolding.
It is not something to be
outmanoeuvred or outwitted.
This story is still incomplete,
and our recovery has yet to begin.
That unknowing is part of our pain.
There is wisdom in accepting
the things we cannot change.
But there is strength
in remembering that nothing,
not even what we can't control,
will separate us from your embrace.
Amen.

✝
✝

God in our prayers for Christian unity,
God in our prayers for human unity:
in the humbling of yourself
we were exalted;
in seeing equality with others
we approach something more divine.
May we discover
in the emptying of ourselves
a way to come together
in a fuller human likeness.
Amen.

God of the Fallen Grain

God of persistent widows,
God of eventual justice:
as some sit with the luxury
of reflecting on how much
can be taken for granted,
others add their weight and their voice
to causes that may never
benefit them directly,
but can make it more likely
for rising generations to
experience what all should enjoy.
May we see privilege not
as a reward,
but as a tool
to build a better world.
Amen.

✝
✝

God of the home we know,
God of the home we seek:
we give thanks
that a part of the human condition
is the hope, the sense,
the lingering feeling
that even though this world
is not as it should be,
a better world exists,
a different future is available,
a home for all of us
waits for all of us,
and today can be a part
of getting there.
Amen.

✝
✝

God of tunnelling roots,
God of winter growth:
beneath the surface,
and when the light is less available,
the trees and shrubs use their time
to strengthen themselves.
Reaching out and feeling forward,
they connect themselves
more assuredly to their surroundings.
May we use this time
in a similar way,
so the spring that arrives
finds us already in fuller bloom.
Amen.

✝
✝

God of the lilies,
God of the ravens:
the wildflowers are having
an absolute field day;
the rabbits can't believe their luck.
Left to do what she does best,
nature certainly shows off.
We, too, may see
which root emotion
will rise and come to flower.
We pray that instead
of the worry the world
has tried to plant,
it may be the hope
you sow inside.
Amen.

✝
✝

God of human touch,
God of spiritual embrace:
this biggest event of our lives
will live on in our tissues,
something our bodies
are actively learning to hold.
And so the kindness we show
to ourselves,
and the support we offer each other,
is not just for right now.
May the soothing techniques we practise
and the centring breaths we take
hold us in this moment
and train us for moments to come,
so that without thinking
we can find ourselves
again in your presence.
Amen.

✝
✝

God of grace and beauty,
God of the crooked shore:
we give you thanks for those
who reveal your grace with
a wisdom they wear so lightly,
in a strength they only use
to lift up other people.
The generosity that some show
in conversation, and in lessons
they impart through open silence,
provides a glimpse of
divine light to be found
in stories yet to be told,
in questions we still want to ask.
Amen.

✝
✝

God of a mother's instinctive compassion;
God whose piety is an impulse to kindness:
our societies are reflections
of ourselves.
The brokenness we lament
out there in the world
mirrors all the fractures within.
May your maternal instinct to redeem us,
through lessons of repentance
and forgiveness,
restore the bonds between us,
so we can reveal both the hurt
and the healing.
And then, may a love
like her love at our birth
begin our new life together.
Amen.

✝
✝

God of early morning birdsong,
God of creatures creating their future:
there is a seasonal rhythm
and a yearly pattern
that points to a continual cycle.
We give thanks that this
is more than simple repetition,
or perpetual sameness.
There is this forward drive,
a pull into coming days
fuelled by hope and possibility,
a desire to be a part of something more;
the instinct to build a nest
for a life that's yet to come.
Amen.

God of the psalms of joy,
God of the psalms of sorrow:
we note that part of being human
is acknowledging the brokenness,
in the world and in ourselves;
and that part of being human
is to love ourselves as you do,
and to recreate
from all the broken bits
a new us and a new world.
Amen.

✝
✝

God of the chaos we fear,
God of the day we create:
the eternal nature of your love
is something greater than permanence.
We don't so much rest upon it
because it is fixed and unchanging
as we continually discover it:
surprising and true.
Give us faith not in what
we hope can still last
from the first breath of creation,
but in what arrives
in this newborn moment:
your voice bringing light
with news that is good.
Amen.

✝
✝

God of bursting early bulbs,
God of links to last year's growth:
stored within us
are lessons and corrections,
surprising revelations and
moments still taking on meaning.
As we open ourselves up
to a new spring,
may we display the colours
we've hidden inside;
and may the rooted life
we hold in our core
ground us well for all
coming seasons.
Amen.

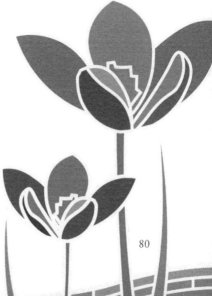

✝
✝

God of the desert and God of the garden:
your son went into the wilderness.
And there he sat.
And there he prayed.
And there he dreamed
of a life more abundant for others.
As we root down for an uncertain time,
and sit with unanswerable questions,
may we sprout new thoughts
for those less able to rest,
so that when we do leave this desert,
we join others in a garden that thrives.
Amen.

✝
✝

God of the fallen grain,
God of the children of light:
it was in your being broken down
that you were lifted up.
It is in releasing our lives to others
that we bear your lasting truth.
As a community dispersed,
may our relinquishing of self,
and our selfless love for others
broadcast wide the great good news
that even in death there is glorious new life,
and that darkness will not overcome it.
Amen.

Acknowledgements

I am very grateful to the Corrymeela Community for embodying welcome, respect, courage and hope for so many; and to the members and staff who contributed directly to this project by selecting and proofreading the prayers we included. I am in debt to Connie Hunter-Jamison at Studio Stereo for her brilliant design and her visual storytelling. She had gorgeous art to work with, and for that we thank Seán Harvey, whose evocative pieces repeatedly stunned us. This book simply would not have happened without Bronagh Vos's vision and drive; the elements that readers particularly like are no doubt due to Bronagh. But it's Kiran, Eva, Amos and Phoebe who receive the bulk of my thanks for the enduring hope they provide.

With gratitude for this latest generation, we dedicate this book to all our parents.

God of the Fallen Grain